Real Life: Superheroes

Written by Alison Hawes

Contents

What is a Superhero?

Comic-book superheroes are lucky enough to have amazing powers, such as super strength or the ability to fly. Some have special equipment, such as Green Lantern's power ring or Iron Man's armour suit. These things help fictional superheroes to make a difference.

Real-life superheroes have a much harder task. They don't have any superpowers to help them. Instead they must rely on *inner* strengths, such as determination and bravery, in order to help others.

Comic-book superheroes are just fictional but there are real-life superheroes who make a big difference to people's lives.

A superhero is someone who makes a difference in the world; someone who is looked up to and respected for helping others.

Making a Stand

Real-life superheroes are brave because they stand up for beliefs that other people don't share. They may risk being laughed at, or even get into trouble for what they believe in. The important thing is that this does not stop real-life superheroes from achieving their goals.

Some real-life superheroes will even risk going to prison in their efforts to make a change. Emmeline Pankhurst was arrested several times as she **campaigned** to win the right for women to vote.

Changing the World

The real-life superheroes in this book all put up with **ridicule**, danger or abuse to make the world a better place to live in. The effects of their world-changing work are still felt today.

Richard Martin

FACT FILE

- **Full name:** Richard Martin
- **Date of birth:** 15th January 1754
- **Nationality:** Irish
- **Died:** 6th January 1834
- **Interests:** horse riding, sailing and going to the theatre
- **Worked:** as an MP (Member of Parliament)
- **Famous for:** getting the world's first animal **welfare** laws passed by Parliament

" Animals ... [are] ... entitled ... to be treated with kindness and humanity ... **"**
Richard Martin

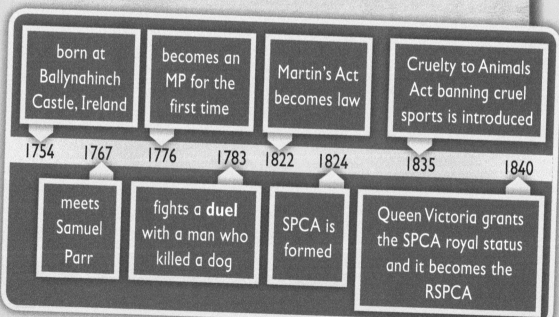

| 1754 | 1767 | 1776 | 1783 | 1822 | 1824 | 1835 | 1840 |

1754 born at Ballynahinch Castle, Ireland

1767 meets Samuel Parr

1776 becomes an MP for the first time

1783 fights a **duel** with a man who killed a dog

1822 Martin's Act becomes law

1824 SPCA is formed

1835 Cruelty to Animals Act banning cruel sports is introduced

1840 Queen Victoria grants the SPCA royal status and it becomes the RSPCA

A Love of Animals

Richard Martin was the oldest child of Robert Martin, a wealthy Irish landowner. As a child, Richard was very fond of animals and hated to see them badly treated.

A Life in Politics

Richard's father wanted him to be a MP when he grew up and sent him to England to be educated. When he was just 22 years old, Richard became an MP for the first time.

Two people in particular inspired Richard's interest in animals and their welfare: his mother and one of his teachers, Samuel Parr.

Richard was an MP in the Irish Parliament, in Dublin. In later years, he was an MP in the House of Commons, in England.

5

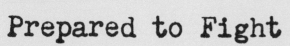

Prepared to Fight

As an MP, Richard was known for his great sense of humour, which often had the other MPs in fits of laughter. Equally, Richard was known for settling disagreements in his private life by fighting duels.

Once, he fought a duel against a man who deliberately killed a friend's dog. Both men were injured in the duel, but Richard felt he had taught the man a lesson he would never forget.

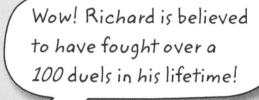

Wow! Richard is believed to have fought over a 100 duels in his lifetime!

In the 18th century a duel was an accepted way of settling an argument, especially between men from wealthy families.

Handing Out Punishment

In 1794, Richard's father died, leaving his land to Richard. Richard also **inherited** the right to hold a local court on the land. Richard surprised his **tenants** by using the court to punish any of them who mistreated their farm animals. Richard usually fined his tenants but sometimes he imprisoned them for a few days on an island on his estate instead!

Richard wanted all the animals on his land to be treated kindly.

In the 18th and early 19th century, some people were naturally kind to their animals but many were not. Many people beat or starved their animals, without thinking they were doing anything wrong.

7

Changing Opinions

During his career as an MP, Richard tried to persuade his fellow MPs that it was wrong to mistreat animals. He wanted them to support a law that would make cruelty to animals a crime.

Richard wanted to stop cruel sports, like **bear-baiting**.

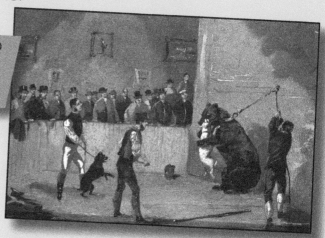

At first, most people just laughed at Richard's ideas. Few people thought animals had feelings or needed any laws to protect them. However, like many real-life superheroes, Richard kept trying to change their minds. Slowly but surely he got more people on his side.

Cartoons making fun of Richard and his beliefs appeared in the newspapers. He was often shown with donkey's ears!

The Terrible Paragraph!! or DICKEY Donkey's Dream is all my Eye and Betty MARTIN.

Outlawing Mistreatment

It took Richard many years but in 1822, when he was 68 years old, he finally managed to get Parliament to pass some of the first laws in the world to protect animals. These laws were known as Martin's Act. They made it illegal to beat or mistreat cattle and other farm animals. This was a great success for Richard and his supporters but Richard wanted more. He wanted a law that banned cruelty to *all* animals.

donkey's owner

Richard Martin

Richard accused a man of mistreating a donkey. He surprised the court by having the donkey brought into the room, so everyone could see its injuries for themselves!

Royal Approval

Two years after Martin's Act was passed, Richard helped to form the Society for the Prevention of Cruelty to Animals (SPCA) to bring people who were cruel to animals to court. The Society was so well thought of that Queen Victoria granted it royal status and it became the Royal Society for the Prevention of Cruelty to Animals (RSPCA). This charity still fights for animal welfare today.

One of the many people inspired by Richard was William Wilberforce MP. William is better known for his campaign against slavery. However, he was also a great supporter of Richard's work and a member of the SPCA.

Changing the Face of Animal Welfare

As a result of the work that Richard began, anti-cruelty laws and animal welfare groups were introduced around the world. Millions of animals have benefited from his determination to make a difference to the way they are treated.

A year after Richard's death, laws were passed banning cruelty to cats and dogs, and cruel sports such as bear-baiting.

Thomas Barnardo

FACT FILE

- **Full name:** Thomas John Barnardo
- **Date of birth:** 4th July 1845
- **Nationality:** Irish
- **Died:** 19th Sept 1905
- **Interests:** reading, writing and preaching
- **Worked as:** a doctor and a social worker with poor children
- **Famous for:** improving the lives of tens of thousands of poor children in Victorian times

❝ **The Father of Nobody's Children** **❞**
W.T. Stead

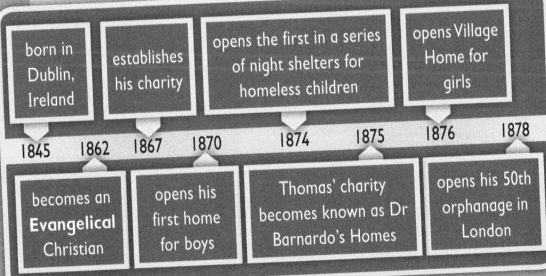

born in Dublin, Ireland	establishes his charity		opens the first in a series of night shelters for homeless children		opens Village Home for girls	
1845	1862	1867	1870	1874	1875	1876	1878
	becomes an **Evangelical** Christian	opens his first home for boys		Thomas' charity becomes known as Dr Barnardo's Homes		opens his 50th orphanage in London

A Troubled Start

Thomas Barnardo was one of four children. He was often very ill as a child, but thankfully he grew up to be fit and strong. Although Thomas was bright and well read, he quickly became bored and often got into trouble at school. He eventually left without passing his exams and went to work as an office worker.

Thomas was born in Dublin.

When he was two years old, Thomas was so ill, he was mistakenly pronounced *dead* by two different doctors!

A New Direction

In his spare time, Thomas began teaching the Bible at a **ragged school** in Dublin, and joined his mother in helping sick and poor people. Then, at the age of 20, he left his job and moved to London to train as a **missionary**.

When Thomas was a teenager, he became an evangelical Christian. Everything he did after that was inspired by his religious beliefs.

Change of Plan

Thomas hoped to qualify as a doctor and then work in China as a medical missionary. However, he never went to China; he found something equally important to do, much closer to home – helping poor children.

Appalling Poverty

As well as studying medicine, Thomas worked at a ragged school in the East End of London. Overwhelmed by the amount of poverty and disease he saw around him, Thomas soon realised that he had found a place where he could work to make a difference. The following year, he set up his own ragged school.

Children being taught at a Victorian ragged school.

In Victorian times, the East End of London was overcrowded and dirty. Many people were unemployed and lived in poverty. Disease was everywhere and thousands were hungry and homeless.

A Shocking Situation

One night, a boy at Thomas' school called Jim Jarvis asked if he could sleep at the ragged school because he had no family or home to go to. Thomas asked to see where Jim lived. That night, Jim showed Thomas where he and many other children slept – on roofs and in dark alleyways, searching for food in all weathers.

Two of the poor and **destitute** children from the East End of London.

The First of Many

Thomas was so affected by the sight of these homeless children that he decided to set up a home where children would get food, shelter and an education. His first home for boys was opened in Stepney in 1870, using money he raised from giving talks and making appeals in newspapers. Homeless children like Jim, were given food, a clean bed and an education.

Thomas spent many nights searching the streets for children in need of a home. This was dangerous work and Thomas was sometimes attacked and robbed.

A Terrible Tragedy

One night a boy called John Somers was turned away from the Stepney Boys' Home because it was full. Two days later, he was found dead in the street. He had died from cold and hunger. Thomas was so devastated that he put a sign on the outside of the home. It read: "No Destitute Child Ever Refused Admission".

A New Venture

Three years after his first home for boys was opened, Thomas married Syrie Elmsie. Syrie shared Thomas' religious beliefs and interest in social work. In 1876, they opened their first home for girls in Barkingside, Essex.

The Barnardo's Girls Village Home in Barkingside was made up of cottages built around a village green.

Plans for Expansion

Thomas was always looking for other buildings to turn into homes and schools for London's poor. In 1877, he opened the biggest ragged school in London, The Copperfield Road Ragged School. Over 300 children were taught here on weekdays and over 2,000 children came to the Sunday school. As well as lessons, the hungry children were given free food.

Hard Work

Where possible, Thomas found foster families for the youngest children he rescued. Older children lived in children's homes until they were old enough to attend a workshop or an industrial school, where they learned a trade before going out to work.

Barnardo's children had a proper childhood, but were also prepared for life as adults.

A Life of Sacrifice

Thomas' work often took him away from his own family. This was difficult for Thomas, but like many superheroes, he often put the happiness of others before his own. When he wasn't busy running his homes and schools, he was raising money to support them. He was the first person to introduce the house-to-house charity collections that we know today.

Thomas raised over £3 million in his lifetime, to support his homes and schools!

A Need to Slow Down

When he was 50 years old, Thomas became ill with a heart condition and he was advised by his doctor to rest. However, Thomas found it hard doing nothing and he returned to working long hours, despite his ill health.

Thomas died at the age of 60. He was given a hero's funeral in Barkingside, where the headquarters of the Barnardo's charity stand today.

Continuing his Care

Thomas founded 96 homes for children in the UK, changing the lives of thousands of poor and destitute children. His charity, Barnardo's, continued this work after his death and still exists today, fighting for the needs and rights of children.

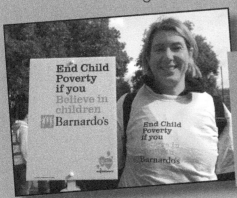

Today, Barnardo's supports over 100,000 children and their families through hundreds of local projects in the UK.

Raoul Wallenberg

FACT FILE

- **Full name**: Raoul Gustav Wallenberg
- **Date of birth**: 4th August 1912
- **Nationality**: Swedish
- **Died**: not known exactly when or how
- **Interests**: drawing, languages and travel
- **Worked as**: a businessman and **diplomat**
- **Famous for**: saving hundreds of thousands of Jewish people in the Second World War

❝The greatest unsung hero of World War II.❞
BBC TV, Man Alive, 1980

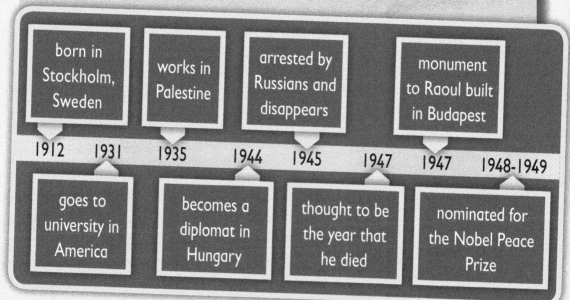

born in Stockholm, Sweden — 1912

goes to university in America — 1931

works in Palestine — 1935

becomes a diplomat in Hungary — 1944

arrested by Russians and disappears — 1945

thought to be the year that he died — 1947

monument to Raoul built in Budapest — 1947

nominated for the Nobel Peace Prize — 1948-1949

A Privileged Upbringing

Raoul Wallenberg was born in Stockholm, three months after his father died. The Wallenbergs were a wealthy banking family and it was expected that Raoul would also beome a banker when he grew up.

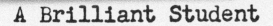

Today a sculpture of Raoul's briefcase marks his birthplace.

A Brilliant Student

Raoul studied hard at school where he showed an interest in drawing and a gift for languages. Later he studied architecture in America but on his return, he was sent to Palestine to train as a banker.

While he was in Palestine, Raoul met many Jews that had escaped from Germany, where Hitler's ruling **Nazi** party was making life very difficult for them. Raoul was shocked by their stories of ill treatment and **persecution**.

A Successful Partnership

Raoul found that banking was not for him and on his return to Sweden, he went into business with a Hungarian Jew called Koloman Lauer. They imported and exported food to different countries in Europe.

The Second World War

When the Second World War broke out, Raoul's business trips took him into **Nazi-occupied** countries, like France, as well as to Germany itself. Here, he was able to see for himself what life was like for Jews under the Nazis.

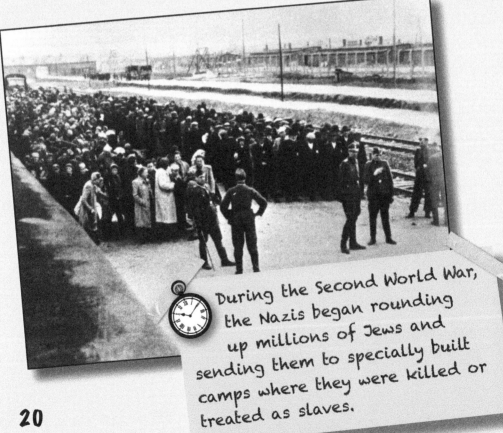

During the Second World War, the Nazis began rounding up millions of Jews and sending them to specially built camps where they were killed or treated as slaves.

A Special Person

In 1944, the Swedish government began looking for someone special to send to Hungary to save as many Jews as they could from the Nazis. Koloman Lauer suggested Raoul for the job, as he was young, brave, eager to help and spoke many languages.

Wow! Raoul could speak Swedish, Russian, English, German and French!

Running Out of Time

Every day, Hungarian Jews were being rounded up, packed on to trains and taken to death camps where they were gassed, shot or worked to death. When Raoul arrived in Hungary, over 40,000 Hungarian Jews had already been **deported** to the death camp at Auschwitz. Raoul had to act quickly to save more people from this fate.

The gates into the death camp at Auschwitz.

Great Ideas

Raoul had special passes made that he gave to the Jews, saying they were under the protection of the Swedish government and must not be deported. Amazingly, he managed to convince the German and the Hungarian authorities that these passes were official legal documents – though this was not strictly true!

This is one of the yellow protective passes that Raoul helped to design.

A Place of Safety

As well as organising protective passes, Raoul set up safe houses where people with his special passes could live. He organised schools, a hospital and kitchens to look after these people and before long, tens of thousands of Jews were crammed into these buildings.

Daring Rescues

Try as he might, Raoul couldn't save everyone. From October 1944, the Nazis increased their campaign against the Jews. Some Jews were arrested or shot, even if they had one of Raoul's special passes. Despite the danger of being killed by Nazi guards, Raoul stopped several trains taking Jews to death camps. Climbing on to the roof, he ordered everyone who had one of his passes out of the trains, and took them back to safety.

A Daring Bluff!

In January 1945, news reached Raoul that everyone held in Budapest's largest Jewish **ghetto** was to be killed. Raoul sent a message to the commander of the German army in Hungary. He said he would personally see that the commander was hanged as a war criminal if he went ahead with the killing! Miraculously, his threat worked and the people were saved.

> **I could never return to Stockholm, knowing that I had failed to do everything within human power to save as many Jews as possible.**
> Raoul Wallenberg

70,000 Hungarian Jews were forced to live behind the locked gates of the Budapest Ghetto during the war.

Increasing Danger

Despite his successes, Raoul began to fear that his life was in danger and he started sleeping at a different house each night to avoid capture.

This memorial in London is one of many in the world that honour the bravery and sacrifice of Raoul.

Unknown Fate

On 17th January 1945, just four months before war ended, Raoul was arrested by advancing Russian soldiers. He was never seen again. For years his family tried to find out what had become of him. Then in 1957, the Russian government finally told them that Raoul had died in prison in 1947. No one can be sure if this is true.

Never Forgotten

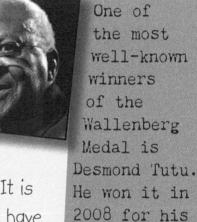

Thousands of people and their families are alive today because of the daring and sacrifice of Raoul. Since 1990, the Wallenberg Medal has been awarded each year in Raoul's memory. It is given to **humanitarians** who, like Raoul, have shown great bravery and determination in helping others.

One of the most well-known winners of the Wallenberg Medal is Desmond Tutu. He won it in 2008 for his life-long work against racism and poverty in South Africa.

Rosa Parks

FACT FILE

- **Full name:** Rosa Louise McCauley Parks
- **Date of birth:** 4th February 1913
- **Nationality:** American
- **Died:** 24th October 2005
- **Interests:** sewing and reading
- **Worked as:** a secretary and a seamstress
- **Famous for:** refusing to give up her seat to a white man on the bus in 1955

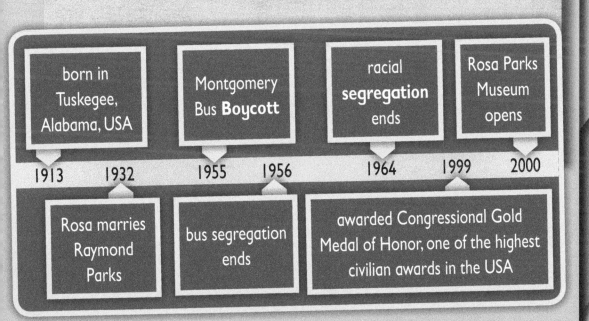

born in Tuskegee, Alabama, USA		Montgomery Bus **Boycott**		racial **segregation** ends		Rosa Parks Museum opens
1913	**1932**	**1955**	**1956**	**1964**	**1999**	**2000**
	Rosa marries Raymond Parks		bus segregation ends		awarded Congressional Gold Medal of Honor, one of the highest civilian awards in the USA	

Difficult Lives

Rosa Parks grew up in the southern USA in the early 20th century. At that time, in America, black and white people lived almost separate lives. In the southern states, the black (or "colored", as it was then called) and the white communities were **segregated** by law.

Signs like these show us how, in almost every part of their lives, black and white citizens were kept separate.

Jim Crow Laws

Under the Jim Crow Laws, both black and white people were supposed to be treated equally, but separately. In reality, white people were given the best jobs and the best schools, while people like Rosa and her family were treated as second-class citizens. Black people were rarely able to vote or earn a decent wage, and were often the target of racial abuse.

Interrupted Education

Rosa's parents split up when she was little and Rosa, her mother and her brother went to live at their grandparents' house. Rosa was taught at home by her mother and didn't go to school until she was 11 years old. She loved school but had to give it up early, to care for her grandmother and her mother, when they became ill.

Rosa went back to school when she was 20 years old to finish her education.

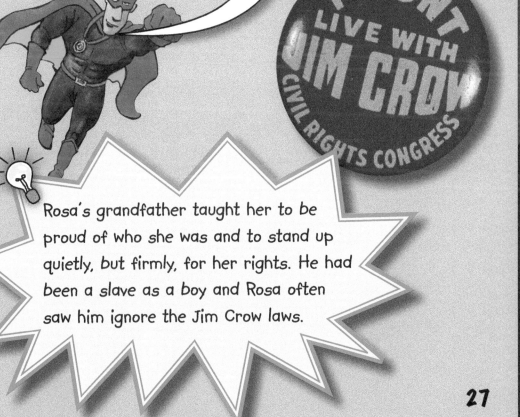

I WON'T LIVE WITH JIM CROW

CIVIL RIGHTS CONGRESS

Rosa's grandfather taught her to be proud of who she was and to stand up quietly, but firmly, for her rights. He had been a slave as a boy and Rosa often saw him ignore the Jim Crow laws.

Civil Rights

Rosa was only 19 years old when she met and married a barber called Raymond Parks. Raymond was already active in the **civil rights** movement. He strongly believed that black people and white people should not be segregated but should be free and equal.

NAACP

Rosa and Raymond joined the National Association for the Advancement of Colored People (NAACP), a civil rights group that campaigned against discrimination based on the colour of a person's skin. Rosa and Raymond were particularly keen to see all black people get the right to vote. By being able to vote, black people could have a say in how the country was run and change its laws for the better. Rosa eventually became secretary of her local NAACP group.

NAACP members campaigned for an end to segregation, especially in schools.

In Montgomery, where Rosa lived, the seats at the front of buses were reserved for white people. Black people had to sit at the back. If the white section was full, the bus driver could order a black person to give up their seat.

Sitting her Ground

One night Rosa caught the bus home from work as usual. She bought her ticket and then went to the back of the bus and sat in the black

section. The white section of the bus soon filled up and when a white man had to stand, the bus driver ordered Rosa to give up her seat. Rosa refused. She knew to refuse was against the law but Rosa believed that it was a bad law. She was tired of being pushed around and always being made to feel second best. The bus driver called the police and Rosa was arrested.

Rosa was photographed and fingerprinted by the police, before being locked in a cell.

Mixed Reactions

After her arrest, Rosa's friends and supporters praised her for her bravery in breaking the law. However, many people were also angered by her actions. Rosa lost her job, her privacy, suffered racial abuse and even death threats. Like many superheroes, Rosa showed great courage throughout this difficult time.

For 381 days, 98% of Montgomery's black citizens joined in the boycott and walked to work.

Bus Boycott

As a protest against the Bus Laws and Rosa's arrest, most black people in Montgomery agreed to stop using the buses. This boycott cost the bus company a lot of money as most of their customers were black. Finally, on 21st December 1956, the Supreme Court in Washington ruled that the buses should no longer be segregated and the boycott ended.

Did you know Rosa had refused to give up her seat before? It was 12 years earlier and she only got thrown off the bus that time!

From a Spark to a Flame

Rosa's refusal to give up her seat on the bus was a very important moment in the history of American civil rights. It was the spark that inspired other civil rights protests in America and abroad, which helped bring racial segregation to an end in the USA.

A Fresh Start

Rosa and Raymond eventually moved to Detroit, where they continued to work for the civil rights movement. Rosa began to receive lots of awards for her work. In 2000, a museum telling her life story was opened on the spot where she had been arrested 45 years earlier.

Rosa died in 2005 when she was 92 years old. Tens of thousands of people attended her funeral.

Glossary

boycott refuse to buy or do something, as a punishment or protest

bear-baiting sport in which dogs are used to attack a bear which has been tied up

campaigned tried to bring about change or raise awareness of an issue

civil rights rights of all people to be treated fairly and equally in society

deported forced to leave a country

destitute without food, shelter or money

diplomat official who represents his own country abroad

duel contest between two people using deadly weapons to settle a point

entitled have the right to do or receive something

evangelical someone who is keen to teach others about their own religion

ghetto part of a city, often a poor area, occupied by a specific group of people

humanitarians people who help others

inherited received money or property from someone after they have died

missionary person who teaches people in other countries about Christianity

Nazi German National Socialist Party who ruled from 1933-1945 led by Adolf Hitler

Nazi-occupied land taken over by German invaders in the Second World War

persecution ill treatment or hostility towards someone

ragged school free schools for poor children

ridicule make fun of

segregation separation by law

tenants people who rent their home or land

welfare health, happiness and fortune

Index